# Contents

# Foreword

As a young probationary teacher in my first year of teaching, I remember hearing an unusual noise which broke the quiet atmosphere during a classroom test. I soon located the source.

Standing confidently in front of Matthew Flint*, the Year 7 student responsible, I was surprised to see that his head remained down and he continued to use his compass point to carve out his name on the wooden desk.

Clearing my throat and using my standing position to exaggerate my presence, I said in my most assertive tone, *'Matthew, what do you think you are doing?'*
Matthew looked up, appeared to conduct a brief survey of the situation, said, *'Go away'* and returned to his task.

I have learned in over 22 years in teaching that although all children are challenging to some extent, some are more challenging than others.

*\* Name has been changed*

# Foreword

The majority of children we could call traditional learners (TLs). They follow the curriculum, behave predictably, and adapt compliantly to the discipline and demands of school. 'TLs' attend regularly and are generally productive for up to 6 hours a day, 5 days a week, 200 plus days a year. In addition, they follow directions and read and respond to the signals that help develop meaningful relationships with their teachers and peers.

But there is another group of children for whom the school experience does not work quite so well; let's call them 'non-traditional learners' or 'NTLs'. These children, perhaps 5 – 10% of the student population, seem to me to be at least 'very uncomfortable' within the educational system. They find the process of learning and conforming far more difficult than others and they're 'challenging' because they take up 90 to 95% of your time, much of it in relation to behavioural issues.

Over the years I have become extremely interested in the behaviour of NTLs. They can be frustrating and difficult to teach. They are often unpredictable. During any incident on any given day (whether it's windy or not!) they may explode, or smile, or laugh at teacher intervention. Worse still, like Matthew, they may simply ignore it.

# Foreword

To manage children with challenging behaviour we need to understand the message behind the behaviour. Why don't these students learn like others? Is it that they can't, that they won't or that they don't care? The following pages look at Attention Deficit Hyperactivity Disorder, Oppositional Defiant Disorder and Conduct Disorder – three conditions that help explain why some children can be so unpredictable, uncooperative, angry and aggressive.

One definition of the word 'challenging' is *'difficult but stimulating'* and this is certainly true of many of the children I have worked with over the years and who I meet in classrooms today. I have found the rewards of working with challenging children far outweigh the difficulties. There is no greater satisfaction than seeing those who are defiant, disruptive, easily distracted (and even, sometimes, dangerous) adapt successfully to the demands of the school system. Getting these children to believe in you – and better still to believe in themselves – is something you can't place a value on. It can be a tricky path to follow, but it's a journey well worth taking.

If you work with children who **can't, won't, or don't**, this Pocketbook will begin the process of understanding what **can, will and does** work.

**Introduction**

 **The Risk Factors**

 **Can't Learn: ADHD**

 **Won't Learn: ODD**

 **Don't Care: CD**

 **The 5Ps: Marketing Good Behaviour**

 **Further Information**

# Introduction

# Main behavioural challenges

Behavioural challenges for the teacher range from major issues of safety and security in the classroom to low-level disruptive factors such as lateness, tardiness and poor organisational skills. They include:

- Physical abuse towards others
- Verbal abuse towards others
- Damage to property
- Challenging authority/rules
- Work/task avoidance
- Poor timekeeping

A key point is that the behaviour exhibited is sending out a message to the observer. By understanding the message behind the behaviour, we can begin to understand how to manage it.

# The message

Without doubt some children like to feel in control or need to feel as if they have power over others. Whether this is a result of nature, nurture or both is open to discussion. Children may misbehave for the following reasons:

- To gain status
- To gain peer approval
- To gain attention
- To avoid work (too easy/hard, boredom)
- They are not used to adults setting appropriate boundaries

Though **nurture** – or, in some cases, lack of it – can account for these and for issues such as aggression and poor self-esteem/self-worth, there is always the possibility of **nature**, as in neurological disorders, playing its part too.

Whichever, the net result is that teaching and learning will usually be adversely affected.

# Characteristics

Although the following characteristics are not exclusive to non-traditional learners, these kinds of children are more likely to:

- Be unhappy, unwilling and/or unable
- Achieve less praise through their work
- Have fewer positive adult interactions
- Have learning difficulties or be underachieving
- Have poor social skills and few friends
- Have poor self-regard
- Be emotionally volatile
- Be easily hurt or upset by others

It's worth repeating three words from the first bullet point above: 'Unhappy', 'Unwilling', 'Unable'. Our goal is to enable children to be:

## HAPPY, WILLING and ABLE.

# Labels

Many diagnostic labels exist to provide specific information on the differences between particular children and to try to explain why certain individuals behave as they do in relation to their teachers and peers within the school community.

Diagnostic labels such as Specific Learning Difficulties (SpLD) and Autistic Spectrum Disorder (ASD) are well established, and present challenges for both teachers and learners. Though these conditions are often an issue for non-traditional learners, they will not form the main focus of this Pocketbook.

# Specific Learning Difficulties (SpLD)

Briefly, Specific Learning Difficulties include **dyslexia**, **dyspraxia** and **dyscalculia**. These three conditions often overlap and cover a range of reading, writing and mathematical difficulties.

**Connected to (but not the main cause of) challenging behaviour, SpLD issues are NOT the main focus of this book.**

## SpLD

DYSLEXIA

DYSPRAXIA

DYSCALCULIA

# Autistic Spectrum Disorder (ASD)

Autistic Spectrum Disorder children have a triad of impairment in these key areas:

- Communication: resulting in language impairment
- Imagination: resulting in rigidity and inflexibility
- Socialisation: resulting in poor social timing and lack of empathy

As these features can vary from severe to mild, the concept of a spectrum exists. Aspergers Syndrome, for instance, appears at the milder end, where children can be extremely high functioning and possess good language skills but may experience difficulties in both imagination and socialisation.

**Connected to (but not the main cause of) challenging behaviour, ASD issues are NOT the main focus of this book.**

# SEBD

The main label given to students who are particularly challenging is the ever-expanding Social, Emotional and Behavioural Difficulties, formerly known as EBD, (which some of us in the field used to refer to as 'Extremely B***** Difficult, Every B***** Day'). The word 'social' is a relatively recent addition.

SEBD has become a general classification for a series of specific sub-groups including:

- Attention Deficit Hyperactivity Disorder (ADHD)
- Oppositional Defiant Disorder (ODD)
- Conduct Disorder (CD)

**Though SEBD overlaps with other conditions such as SpLD and ASD, the issues within SEBD are the MAIN focus for this book.**

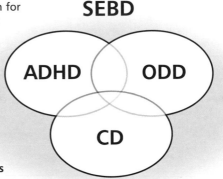

# Three main types of SEBD

$$SEBD = ADHD + ODD + CD$$

Though there are a number of different categories of challenging children, the following chapters deal with three main types:

- Those that **can't** learn but generally **want** to  (ADHD)
- Those that **won't** learn but **might** if it's on their terms (ODD)
- Those that **don't** care; they appear to have a different agenda (CD)

$$SEBD = can't + won't + don't\ care$$

# A classroom scenario

Consider the following situation: the teacher Miss Maple is working from the board and behind her back a pen is thrown across the room. She turns around and eyes up three individuals she feels might be involved: Liam, Vicky and Darren.

## The case for Liam

Liam is looking really uncomfortable, shifting both on his seat and his gaze when Miss Maple looks at him. Twiddling his tie, he looks helplessly along at the boy sitting next to him, Darren. Darren ignores both Liam and the teacher.

*'Liam,'* says the teacher.

*'Yes Sir…. I mean Miss,'* says Liam. *'What did I do?'*

*'I didn't say you did anything,'* says Miss Maple, *'but a pen was thrown across the room.'*

*'It wasn't me Sir… I mean Miss. I don't have many pens left… I lost most of them. Was it one of mine?'* he asks.

# A classroom scenario

## The case for Vicky

*'Vicky,'* says Miss Maple, but before she can finish…

*'You don't think I did it,'* says Vicky shouting. *'Why are you always picking on me? You never leave me alone. I never even touched your stupid pen.'*

*'Vicky,'* Miss Maple begins, but before she can finish…

*'Why do you always blame me for everything? You have 29 other kids in here but it's always me. If you would concentrate on making the lesson more interesting and not so boring perhaps people wouldn't go around chucking pens anyway.'*

# A classroom scenario

## The case for Darren

Darren is texting on his phone and ignores the first request that Miss Maple makes to him.

*'Darren do you know anything about the pen that was thrown across the room a few minutes ago? And by the way, please put that phone away.'*

*'No, why should I?'* he says. *'It's nothing to do with me.'*

*'Are you sure?'* asks Miss Maple. *'It came from this direction.'*

*'Did it?'* says Darren flippantly. *'But how do you know? You had your back turned. Anyway, didn't Liam say it was one of his? Look, here's mine.'*

**So...** Which of the three students, Liam, Vicky and Darren best fits the 'can't learn, won't learn, don't care' criteria and why?

# The verdict

Difficult though it is to create stereotypes, from the three students profiled:

Liam is likely to be regarded as the **can't learn** student. He comes across as the type who does not think about the implications or consequences of their actions and who would not have thought through the throwing of the pen.
**Students with ADHD often fit into this category.**

Vicky is likely to be regarded as the **won't learn** student as she is potentially explosive when asked about the incident. Her fragile temperament leads her to challenge the teacher almost before she knows it. It is this secondary behaviour that gets her into most hot water.
**Students with ODD often fit into this category.**

Darren is typical of the **don't care** student; his actions are more premeditated and controlled than the other two and he is more calculating in his responses.
**Students with CD are more likely to fit into this category.**

# The culprit?

As for who actually threw the pen, it could have been any one of them but the example demonstrates three things:

1. Students with ADHD are usually the easiest to catch as they are impulsive. Because they do not plan in advance, they will not have an alibi for their behaviour. (They may try to lie but they are poor liars because in addition to their impulsiveness they have poor short-term memory.)

2. Students with ODD are more difficult to catch after the act than those with ADHD but easier than those with Conduct Disorder. However, be warned: by the time you have proved their complicity they will have twisted the story so much that they'll have convinced you it was your fault – the lesson was so boring they threw the pen to liven it up.

3. Students with Conduct Disorder do plan and are difficult to catch. They generally do have an alibi, usually the student with ADHD sitting beside them!

Introduction

 The Risk Factors ◀

 Can't Learn: ADHD

 Won't Learn: ODD

 Don't Care: CD

 The 5Ps:
Marketing
Good Behaviour

 Further
Information

# The Risk Factors

# The child, the family, the community

So why do certain children exhibit inappropriate behaviours when others do not?

There are a number of key risk factors which can affect children. We can break these down into issues inherent in:

 The child (pages 23-27)

 The family (pages 28-33)

 The community (page 34)

#  The child

Starting with the first of these, risk factors inherent in **the child** might include:

- Specific learning difficulties/neurological difficulties
- Levels of intelligence, IQ and emotional intelligence
- Difficult temperament
- Physiological issues – levels of self-esteem, depression, stress

Obviously, specific learning difficulties – dyslexia, for instance – do not necessarily lead to challenging behaviour but they may be a factor in contributing towards frustration and poor self-esteem in school.

Similarly, level of intelligence might not be a direct cause of inappropriate behaviour but it can be a contributory factor.

Poor levels of emotional intelligence, however, very often lead to children finding it difficult to read the signals necessary for positive social interaction. Such students struggle to share or wait their turn and often are extremely inflexible, especially when under stress.

#  Emotional intelligence

Daniel Goleman defines emotional intelligence as 'the capacity to process emotional information accurately and effectively, including the capacity to perceive, assimilate, understand and manage emotion'. He identifies five key areas:

- Knowing your emotions
- Managing your emotions
- Motivating yourself
- Recognising emotion in others
- Handling relationships

It is often said that children with autism have poor EI and the same is true for students with SEBD, especially those in the 'don't care' category, who exhibit extremely low levels of empathy. This lack of empathy and inability to feel emotion can make it very difficult to help children reflect on their actions and thereby improve future conduct.

Specialised training, which may include strategies such as visual stories and role-play, is often needed to help individuals with poor EI understand the impact of their behaviour.

#  Temperament

Are children born with it or does temperament develop? Well, the truth probably lies somewhere between the two. Having said that, mothers tell me that the day their babies were born they could tell whether they were likely to be happy or unhappy individuals.

In one family of non-identical twin boys well known to this author, it was clear from the outset that one of the twins was 'half full' in his personality while the other was 'half empty'.....

The second twin's first three words were: *'It's not fair'* – a reflection of things to come.

#  Temperament

The point is that certain children will be more difficult to work with because they will see the negative side of every issue. They may be moody, unpredictable and sometimes explosive. You'll feel like you're walking on eggshells when working with them.

The most important thing for such students is to get them to feel that you realise when they're having a bad day. Though it may not stop incidents occurring, it will lessen the impact and will go towards developing a positive relationship with them, which is the key to managing a difficult temperament.

# ☉ Self-esteem, depression, stress

Whatever lies behind poor self-esteem, depression and stress amongst children, the fact remains that these are real issues that will, in some cases, need a range of options beyond teacher intervention.

Self-esteem is linked to self-confidence, so any strategies teachers can use to banish the fear of failure and boost self-image are to be recommended. (See the *Dyslexia Pocketbook* by Julie Bennett, for information about raising self-esteem and for creating the climate, relationships and opportunities that promote safe learning.)

Depression and stress in young people may be mild or severe. Finding the cause holds the key to the solution. Teachers should alert the relevant officers within the school community to establish the extent of the problem and thereby access the relevant agencies.

#  The family

Though factors in children themselves can lead to challenging behaviour, there are a number of issues related to **family** that will also affect performance in school. These include:

- Overt parental conflict and family breakdown
- Sibling rivalry
- Death and loss – including loss of friendship
- Inconsistent or unclear discipline
- Hostile or rejecting relationships
- Physical, sexual or emotional abuse
- Parental criminality, alcoholism or personality disorder
- Health of parents

#  The family

Teachers will have little or no influence on family issues but it is, nevertheless, important to look sometimes beyond the behaviour in the classroom to understand the reasons behind it.

Parents divorcing, problems with brothers and sisters, the death of a close relative will all affect children in ways that they will be unable to convey in words. Instead, they will communicate their pain and frustrations through actions, and teachers and other pupils at the school may well be at the sharp end.

In a Teachers' TV survey in October 2005, 750 teachers were asked the main reasons for school behavioural problems:

- **80%** stated lack of parental control
- 37% weak or inconsistent discipline policies
- 25% unimaginative curriculum

Teachers appear fairly convinced that some parents can do a better job.

#  Inconsistent or unclear discipline

There is no doubt that parenting is the most difficult job in the world. One thing is clear, though: children need parents to be parents.

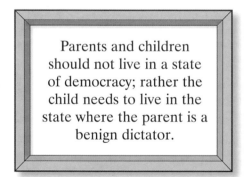

Parents and children should not live in a state of democracy; rather the child needs to live in the state where the parent is a benign dictator.

#  Inconsistent or unclear discipline

However unpopular this statement might be, I don't think it is possible to avoid saying: *'Some children are plainly unlucky with the parents they have'*. Though all parents love their children, some, for a range of reasons, are not always good role models.

Talking about a particular troubled boy, one teacher said, *'At home Shafiq gets the best of everything and the worst of everything.'*

When I asked what he meant he explained: *'One minute his Dad comes in in a good mood and says, 'Shafiq you're a good boy' and gives him a mobile phone as a gift. 30 minutes later, while the family are watching TV, Shafiq's phone goes off and Dad rushes over to Shafiq and cuffs him around the head saying, 'Turn that \*\*\*\*\*\*\* phone off, I'm watching TV.'*

**No consistency at home will leave Shafiq inconsistent at school and elsewhere.**

 # An unfortunate truth

A dentist visiting a school recently and handing out free toothbrushes to a group of year 4 students noticed that one of the boys had not taken a brush. When the dentist asked why he'd not taken one, the boy shrugged his shoulders, so the dentist asked, *'What colour would you like?'* The boy shrugged his shoulders again. The dentist persisted, *'What colour is your toothbrush at home?'*

*'I don't have a toothbrush at home,'* the boy replied.

Every child, especially when they are young, thinks their Mummy and Daddy are the best Mummy and Daddy in the world...

Some of those children are wrong.

 # Young carers

In a TES report the following facts about young carers were made:

- There is likely to be at least one young carer in every school, some as young as five
- Most are caring for parents (usually a mother) for between one and 19 hours a week, but nearly 1,000 five to seven-year-olds are caring for more than 50 hours a week
- Tiredness, anxiety and poor attendance can contribute to low attainment
- One in three young carers is missing schooling. A quarter have no GCSEs
- About 80% emotionally support a family member, more than the number who cook, clean and shop

Children involved as carers are probably not going to behave in a traditional way. They may be regularly missing from classes or, if in school, preoccupied with other responsibilities.

This is a good example of how, by looking behind the behaviour, we can understand the message it may be sending. In cases like these the teachers' role is to make sure the relevant school officers are informed so that support mechanisms can be put in place.

#  The community

Although **community** factors, such as wealth or lack of it, do not necessarily *cause* challenging children, they can be a contributory element, especially where families are finding it difficult to deal with specific circumstances. Community factors include:

- Socio-economic disadvantage
- Constant change of circumstances
- Homelessness
- Disaster
- Discrimination
- Other significant life events

Schools may not be able to counteract many of these community issues, but they can at least play a role in stamping out discrimination and prejudice which, if unchecked, can lead to bullying and have lasting effects on targeted individuals.

One teacher I know uses the 3Ns in his classroom management of the 3Bs (the bullies, the bullied and the bystanders):

**Not here; Not now; NEVER...**

Introduction

 The Risk Factors

  Can't Learn: ADHD ◀

 Won't Learn: ODD

 Don't Care: CD

 The 5Ps:
Marketing
Good Behaviour

 Further
Information

# Can't Learn:
# ADHD

# Attention Deficit Hyperactivity Disorder

Attention Deficit Hyperactivity Disorder (ADHD) is also sometimes known as Attention Deficit Disorder or ADD.

One mother told me it stood for 'Attention Devastation Disorder', as this was the impact on her life. A girl, after being told that this was her condition, believed she had heard that she had 'tense and deaf orders'.

In reality, children with ADHD have a triad of impairment. The three core symptoms are:

**Inattention**    **Impulsivity**    **Hyperactivity**

'Devastation' is just one of many 'D words' that might be applied to those with ADHD; some of the others are: demanding, disruptive, defiant and most definitely different.

Children with ADHD are a challenge for most classroom teachers.

# Attention Deficit Hyperactivity Disorder

Within the term ADHD (see Appendix 1), three sub-types exist:

- Predominantly Inattentive Type (PIT)
- Hyperactive Impulsive Type (HIT)
- Combined Type (CT)

Predominantly inattentive type children are those who appear listless and, though not usually physically hyperactive, are mentally hyperactive. In another generation they might have been classified as 'space cadets'. Not usually associated with anti-social behaviour, these children are more prone to low self-esteem, depression, anxiety and, in extreme cases, self-harm. They are definitely an 'at risk' group.

The other two sub-groups, the Hyperactive Impulsive Type and Combined Type will often be challenging, demanding and disruptive, both inside and outside the classroom. They will be a 'risk-taking' group.

# Signs

ADHD is said to affect 3 to 5% of the child population. It is considered to be a medical condition, often with a strong hereditary factor. It is a recognised mental health condition and is covered by disability discrimination law, which states that every school has a duty to cater for students' individual needs whether or not they are statemented and/or diagnosed. In 2008 the UK National Institute of Clinical Excellence stated:

- **ADHD is a real and genuine condition**
- **A range of measures including educational and behavioural strategies can improve the outcomes of children with ADHD**

- **Medication can and should be used to improve the outcomes of individuals who suffer with ADHD symptoms**

For teachers in the classroom, some key indicators of a child with ADHD are:
- Has trouble paying attention
- Fails to finish things he/she starts
- Spacey/daydreams
- Frequently calls out/acts impulsively
- Has trouble completing assigned work
- Has difficulty in staying organised
- Is restless/overactive

The key element, however, is that individuals with ADHD act without thinking:

'The first time I think about it is too late – I have already done it.'

# Signs in girls

Though fewer in numbers than boys, girls with ADHD have the following characteristics:

- Their problems are frequently under-appreciated
- They may be inattentive only
- By adolescence they may be depressed/have low self-esteem/be learning disabled

It is often thought that girls are under-diagnosed with ADHD compared with their male counterparts as *'boys make the most noise'*. Boys with high levels of testosterone-fuelled 'disruptive' hyperactivity tend to be seen as having difficulties, whereas girls with a similar but less boisterous form are more often seen as 'dizzy' rather than disruptive.

Girls with PIT are easily overlooked, especially at primary school. There is evidence to suggest that their 'spacey', unassertive personalities place them at risk of bullying and, as a result, of secondary issues, such as depression, leading to self abuse/harm.

Girls with ADHD are an 'at risk' group. Look out for them and learn what the signs are telling you. What message is being sent by the girl sitting in the corner in Year 4 playing with her hair while all the others are talking in a group?

# Diagnosis

Making sure that a child's behaviour is a result of ADHD requires specialised testing which will include the following areas:

- Medical evaluation
- Parent interview
- Teacher interview
- Child interview
- Rating scales
- Computerised testing
- Achievement testing
- Intellectual testing

Testing is usually conducted by a paediatrician or child psychiatrist and, in some cases, a clinical psychologist.

# Diagnosis

For a diagnosis of ADHD to be made, any other medical reasons why children could be impulsive or overactive, (such as sensory impairment or being affected adversely through allergies or even specific foods), will need to be ruled out.

A comprehensive analysis of the history of the child, both at home and school, will be made to establish the age of onset of the behaviours and the factors affecting them.

Finally, computerised testing can assess attention to detail and vigilance, whilst achievement testing can provide evidence of the academic potential of the child compared with their – in most cases – lower academic performance.

When I'm asked, *'Does ADHD really exist?'* my answer is:

*'At this time, ADHD is the best way of explaining a group of specific behaviours that cannot be better explained by any other means.'*

# What does a child with ADHD look like?

# Response inhibition

Though ADHD is a well-established learning difficulty, scientists continue to debate why children and adults are affected in this way. One theory is that individuals with ADHD, as well as having problems with attention, are unable to inhibit or control their responses in the way that traditional learners do, leading to impulsive actions and verbal responses.

This lack of 'screening', the inability to hesitate before responding to people or particular situations, can lead to a great deal of difficulty for those with ADHD and for the people working with them.

**'Got to say it, got to say it now.'**

# Are children with ADHD always impulsive or hyperactive?

As for whether children with ADHD are *always* impulsive or hyperactive, the simple answer is no. The condition can, therefore, be difficult to diagnose and frustrating for teachers, who will occasionally see their ADHD students extremely focused and involved.

Michael Gordon, an American health professional, sums things up:

'Their behaviour will vary according to the degree to which rules are managed, the amount of structure and support for compliance and the degree to which the child is interested in the activity.'
**(Dr. Michael Gordon,1992.)**

# Distract them

Children with ADHD are extremely sensitive to the person teaching them.

One of the most effective teachers of children with ADHD I have been aware of over the years was a strapping teacher with a booming voice. He had a great deal of presence and a unique line for children who weren't listening to him:

*'Pay attention or I will eat you.'*

It's an approach you're unlikely to find recommended in teacher-training manuals but you can see how it might hold the interest of students with ADHD, who need stimulation at all times!

Both this example and Dr. Gordon's comment on page 44 make the same point. Students with ADHD are easily distracted. The trick is to exploit this and find ways of distracting them from the person beside them and from thoughts in their heads, towards the learning process.

# Classroom problems associated with ADHD

Although not unique to ADHD, many of the typical characteristics of this disorder relate to high energy, impulsiveness and lack of concentration skills:

- Being frequently out of seat at inappropriate times and in inappropriate situations
- Deviating from what the rest of the class is supposed to do
- Not following instructions (teachers' or assistants')
- Talking out of turn or calling out
- Being aggressive towards classmates
- Having a short attention span and being easily distracted
- Bothering classmates, hindering them in their work efforts
- Being oblivious and day-dreaming
- Losing and forgetting equipment
- Producing work that is incomplete or sloppy

# Multi-modal management

ADHD is a complex condition. Theories abound regarding its causes but most scientists agree that it's caused by neurotransmitter deficiency within the brain. Although medication is not always required, most professionals agree that management of ADHD will require educational, behavioural and physiological input. This is known as a multi-modal approach.

This chapter deals mainly with educational and medical options while more briefly considering the other three. Behaviour modification will be covered in greater detail on pages 99-118 when we look at a collective approach towards the range of challenging children.

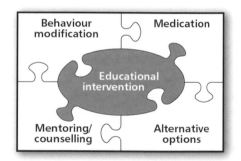

# Expectations and text

When it comes to supporting ADHD children in class, it's generally helpful to reduce your expectations of written work and be prepared to use alternative ways of recording information. Give simple, unambiguous instructions, offer prompts and provide various 'ways in' to the work

Children with ADHD need bright, uncluttered material. It's a case of less is more:

- Review the design of your worksheets and tests. Avoid hand-written worksheets
- Use black print and appropriate-sized clear type. (Sans serif fonts, such as Arial, Comic Sans, Verdana and *Tahoma*, are best)
- Keep format simple – only one or two activities per page
- Avoid unnecessary pictures or visual stimuli
- Ensure white space on each page
- Differentiate as appropriate and provide alternative environments for tests and exams

# Making text accessible

One teacher I worked with noticed that Mani in Year 7 could not focus on his maths multiplication problems. As he said:

*'The page is too busy Miss.'*

The teacher took a file divider and cut a hole in the middle of the page at a size that would equate to each problem and placed it on the sheet of maths questions and said to Mani:

*'Look, there is a window for this page.'*

Mani responded, *'Yep I see it. How many do I have to do?'*

Always be aware that sometimes it is the text or the format of the text provided that is distracting for the child with ADHD. Too many words or too many questions, as in the example given, appear cluttered and distracting. Make text accessible with large, clear print and plenty of space on the page.

# Giving instructions

When giving instructions to ADHD students who find listening difficult:

- Repeat directions individually and encourage students to repeat them back to you
- Give an outline of steps to be taken in following instructions, eg: my task, equipment I need, what I will do first, etc
- Use highlighter pens to emphasise directions for students and encourage them to highlight important items too
- Provide a study partner
- Acknowledge student has something to say but help to develop self-control, eg: *'John, I can see that you are itching to give me the answer but I just want to see what Jack has to say about it and I will come back to you'*. Praise if quiet until return

# Activity and structure

ADHD children really need help to concentrate.  Often, having something to do will do the trick. They also respond well to structure.  Try these strategies:

- Allow a calming down period before coming into class
- Encourage a calm atmosphere in class and give short breaks between assignments
- Plan ahead for transition times
- Allow student to fiddle with an agreed object, eg stress ball, concentrators, bar magnets, etc
- Use alternative technology, eg computer, music
- Set a variety of tasks and activities, where possible including 'hands on' activities

Also, consider including whole-class physical stretching exercises midway through lessons. These provide an opportunity for out-of-seat activities for children who find sitting for long periods difficult and they help subsequent concentration.

# Classroom environment

It is not just the materials, approaches and lesson content that teachers need to work with, it's also the classroom environment:

- Identify a safe haven/quiet area in the room
- Seat away from door, window, corridor
- Seat away from resources not in use
- Seat away from resources needed by other students
- Seat near teacher
- Seat near a student who has good study and attention skills
- Use work stations, if available
- Use horseshoe classroom layout for discussion

# ADHD in action

It is crucial in managing
children with ADHD to be
prepared in advance for
situations arising from
children's short
attention spans.

> Be
> *proactive*
> not
> *reactive*

It is often said – and it is true – that the only person's behaviour you can control is
your own. When it comes to other people, you can only influence their actions. The
following two examples illustrate how the behaviour of the teacher can influence the
outcome when dealing with a child with ADHD.

# Being reactive

Taylor is really finding it hard to sit still at his table in the Year 5 class. Renata, his partner, is looking concerned as he is flicking bits of paper across the room at Jermayne and swinging on his chair. He is finding it difficult to concentrate and is not listening to the teacher, who is teaching the class about the Great Plague. Suddenly, he gets out of his chair and shouts out…

*'Ring a ring of roses Miss.'*

*'What?'* says the teacher.

*'Ring a ring of roses Miss… they all fall down.'*

*'Taylor, please sit down and what are you talking about?'*

*'Miss, the Black Plague, that's where the rhyme came from didn't it?'*

*'Yes Taylor, that is true but we are not discussing that today.'*

*'Stop messing Miss about,'* Renata hisses.

*'Whatyasay?'* says Taylor, now trying to touch his nose with his tongue.

# Being proactive

Taylor is really finding it hard to sit still at his table in the Year 5 class. Renata, his partner, is looking concerned as he is flicking bits of paper across the room at Jermayne and swinging on his chair. He is finding it difficult to concentrate and not listening to the teacher, who is teaching the class about the Great Plague. Suddenly he gets out of his chair and shouts out…

*'Ring a ring of roses Miss.'*

*'Taylor, do you have something to add to this lesson?'*

*'Yes Miss, during the Black Plague people died and the…'*

*'OK Taylor, I realise you know something about this period of history. Here's what we will do. Instead of shouting out, I am going to put this special notepad on your desk and every time you think of something about this I want you to jot it down on a note and when you have five notes come up to my table and drop them in my tray. Renata, will you help Taylor remember to do this?'*

*'Yes Miss,'* say Taylor and Renata at the same time.

# Medication

One of the most controversial aspects of ADHD management is the use of medication. How the medication works is beyond the scope of this book, but the fact remains that although medication is not always necessary, because ADHD is a medical condition it may sometimes require a medical intervention.

Though opinions differ on this, the general medical view in the UK is that medication for management of ADHD should be considered only after comprehensive evaluation and if the following conditions prevail:

- The child is at significant risk of harming himself/herself or others
- Earnest attempts at non-medical intervention have proved insufficient
- The child is at risk of emotional and/or academic failure

**Medication does not cure ADHD but it is one of the options available within the multi-modal management model.** (See page 47.)

# Medication

Stimulant medication allows the child to concentrate and pay attention. It's not given because a child is sick, but to help improve the way his or her brain functions. Stimulants work by changing the levels of brain chemicals and making receptors in the brain work more efficiently.  This makes focusing, as well as learning, easier and can help decrease impulsivity.

**Methylphenidate** is by far the most common drug used for medication intervention. It has a controlled drug status and comes in short-acting, intermediate-acting and long-acting pills.

**Ritalin and Equasym** are the brand names for the short-acting methylphenidate.  This medication usually starts working in about 20 minutes. Its effects last for about four hours. Ritalin was first commercially released for use in 1957.  There is extensive research indicating short-term effectiveness, ie 70 to 80% of children with ADHD find it useful.  There is no evidence that it leads to dependency.

Another stimulant called **Dexamphetamine**, brand name **Dexedrine**, is also available. This acts in a similar way to methylphenidate and its effects last for about four hours.

# Medication

There are two long-acting versions of methylphenidate: **Concerta XL** which works for 12 hours and **Equasym XL** and **Medikinet** which both last for 6-8 hours. Another option is the long-acting stimulant **Lisdexamfetamine Dimesylate**, brand name **Elvanse** which also works for 12 hours.

Their advantage is that they cover the whole school day, so the child does not have to take any medication while at school. This can prevent teasing about having to take a 'happy pill' and removes the complication of storing medication in school.

In addition, **Atomoxetine**, which is a non-stimulant and non-controlled medicine, is available for the treatment of ADHD in children and adolescents. It is marketed as **Strattera**. Another available non-stimulant is **Guanfacine**, marketed under the brand name **Intuniv**.

These medications have a direct effect on attention, short-term memory, vigilance, reaction time, listening skills and on-task behaviours. They do not treat associated problems such as oppositional and anti-social behaviours, learning difficulties or emotional immaturity. However, as they improve concentration, they may indirectly have a beneficial effect upon some of these behaviours. Common side effects can include loss of appetite, sleep problems, headaches, and stomach aches.

# Alternative options

Scientific evidence suggests that imbalances or deficiencies of certain highly unsaturated fatty acids (HUFA) may contribute to a range of behavioural and learning difficulties including ADHD, dyslexia, dyspraxia, and autistic spectrum disorders.

These omega-3 and omega-6 fatty acids are found in fish and seafood, some nuts and seeds and green leafy vegetables. They are absolutely essential for normal brain development and function, but research shows that some people may need higher levels in their diet than others.

Food supplements of HUFA may, therefore, help in the management of ADHD. Controlled trials have provided preliminary evidence for this in ADHD and dyslexia, but further treatment trials are still needed.

# Other dietary influences

For many years diet has been said to be one of the major causes of hyperactivity. Giving fizzy drinks to children with ADHD will not help the situation but in most cases it is not a major factor.

Research shows that about 5% of children with ADHD respond in a direct and obvious way to particular substances in their diet. However, healthy eating of regular varied food, which provides a constant blood sugar level through out the day, will be beneficial for all pupils. Children from chaotic homes, where one or other parent may also have a degree of ADHD, may well not be provided with a predictable, nourishing lunchbox. This can be an ongoing challenge.

# Mentoring and counselling

Finally, students with ADHD who are having difficulties in a range of areas in school, at home and with relationships with their peers, need someone to talk to about the challenges they face.

A teacher or learning mentor can be someone on their side, an advocate for them in the often stressful lives they lead. Counsellors may need to be involved, especially with older children who may be suffering from extremely low self-esteem or depression.

# Summary of key strategies for ADHD

In summary:

- Students with ADHD are both easy to distract and distracting. Find ways you can distract them with proactive teaching and management, create opportunities for fidgeting, calling out, etc
- Seating needs to reflect levels of hyperactivity, impulsivity and 'distractibility'
- Set realistic goals and expectations within the classroom in terms of academic and behavioural outcomes
- Consider medication in some cases
- Consider diet and the option of dietary supplements
- Provide the child with an advocate or mentor

# Won't Learn:
# ODD

# Oppositional Defiant Disorder

Oppositional Defiant Disorder (see Appendix 2) often overlaps with both ADHD and CD and covers individuals who present with four core characteristics. They:

- Argue with adults
- Refuse and defy
- Are angry and defensive
- Are spiteful and vindictive

These are the serial arguers, the ones who will never back down and it is never 'their fault'. They can be extremely verbally aggressive in public confrontation. They possess a counter will – the more pressure you apply the greater the opposition you are likely to encounter. If you tell them off they are likely either to explode or smile at you... grrr...the latter can set your blood boiling.

# Managing ODD

Dealing with students with ODD requires a delicate balance of the 3Fs:

- **F**irmness
- **F**airness
- **F**lexibility

Consider the following situation and three different ways in which it could be handled.

The Head of Year 8 notices Mayella in the corridor. It's Mayella's first day back in school following a two-day exclusion for swearing at a teacher. She is wearing black boots when the school uniform code explicitly states that shoes should be worn.

# Managing ODD – situation 1

T: Mayella, what do you think you are doing wearing boots in school? They are not allowed.

A: Boots, boots, why are you going on about stupid boots? I'm just back in school! I sat through Mr Jenkins' stupid class and behaved, despite the fact that he's out to get me excluded again and all you go on about is my boots. You make me laugh.

T: Mayella, this attitude of yours is going to get you excluded again. Is that what you want?

A: What I want is for you to leave me alone and mind your own business.

T: Mayella, that is quite enough. Go to my office right now. You are going home to change. You will not attend this school unless you are in the correct uniform.

A: Go to hell.

*Mayella storms off and kicks the door in front of her.*

# Managing ODD – situation 2

T:  Mayella, what have I told you before about wearing boots to school? They are not allowed.

A:  Boots, boots, why are you going on about stupid boots? I'm just back in school! I sat through Mr Jenkins' stupid class and behaved, despite the fact that he's out to get me excluded again and all you go on about is my boots. You make me laugh.

T:  Well Mayella, I'm not trying to make things difficult for you, but really if I let you wear boots I might have other students wearing boots and then what would I do?

A:  I don't care what you do. What I want is for you to leave me alone and mind your own business.

T:  Well Mayella, that's not fair, but, as I can see that you're in a bad mood I'll talk to you later when you're calmer.

A:  Yeah, whatever.

*Mayella turns her back on the teacher, grins and saunters through the door.*

# Managing ODD – situation 3

T: Mayella, good to see you back in school. Not so good to see you wearing those boots, though.

A: Boots, boots. why are you going on about stupid boots? I'm just back in school! I sat through Mr Jenkins' stupid class and behaved, despite the fact that he's out to get me excluded again and all you go on about is my boots. You make me laugh.

T: Mayella, the rules and the uniform code say shoes should be worn in school and that is what I want you to do.

A: What I want is for you to leave me alone and mind your own business.

T: My business is getting you to be successful in school and when I see you tomorrow I want to see you in shoes. OK?

A: Maybe.

T: Those boots do look fantastic though.

*Mayella looks at her boots, brushes a speck off them and opens the door.*

# Summary

Let's look at the three examples to see how the 3Fs are applied.

In situation 1 the teacher is certainly **firm** but she's somewhat confrontational in her attitude towards what is **fair** regarding all children having to follow the uniform code. Her **inflexibility** in following the rule to the letter inflames the situation, causing Mayella to storm off. The matter is left unresolved.

In situation 2 the teacher tries to be **flexible**, but appealing to an agitated Mayella over the dress code and what is fair amongst the student community dissolves any sense of **firmness** and, consequently, respect for her authority. Mayella clearly thinks this is a weak teacher she can run rings around.

# Summary (cont'd)

In situation 3, however, the teacher provides a good example of how to apply the 3Fs. She starts positively by welcoming Mayella back, but reinforces the rule in a non-confrontational way.

After Mayella's initial explosive outburst, the teacher again reinforces the rule **firmly**, emphasising its **fairness** in the context of the school community.

Despite a second outburst, the teacher remains **firm** but, crucially, she is also **flexible** by not insisting that Mayella go home to change the boots right away, especially as she has only just returned to school after an exclusion.

Finally, this teacher employs a fourth F: she has a bit of **fun**, even in these trying circumstances. Her last comment is most likely to develop a positive relationship between pupil and teacher and bring about a long-term change in behaviour.

# Mood management

Students who have been diagnosed with ODD appear across the age range, but it is often in the moody, unpredictable teenage years that teachers complain the effects are most significant.

True, all teenagers can be moody and difficult to reason with at times, but having ODD creates a 'double whammy' effect. Teenagers with ODD see the world as against them and their moods are very unpredictable.

Although developmental changes, such as growth and hormones, are often said to be the cause of general teenage angst, the results of an interesting study in 2002 might explain why certain individuals appear to think that 'people have it in for them'.

# Mood management

In 2002, McGivern, working with 250 subjects aged from 10 to 22, measured the ability to read facial expressions. He found that teenagers were less able to do this than younger children. 12 year-olds were slowest, only 20% as proficient as 10 year-olds. Only at age 15 did they regain the ability of 10 year-olds.

Add to this the general belief that children with ODD have more difficulty than others in understanding or picking up on traditional social cues and you can see how teenagers with ODD may struggle more than most with reading body language. As a result, they are likely to misinterpret situations and so respond unpredictably or inappropriately.

By contrast, the ability to read the extremely fragile mood of students with ODD is vital if you are to be successful in teaching and managing them. The next few pages cover what to do and what not to do in a potentially explosive situation.

Let's look at Vicky again:

# Mood management – situation 1

*The Teacher scans the classroom and sees Ina turning around and saying something to Vicky two rows behind.*

T:  *(Speaking loudly)* Ina, turn around now.

*Vicky stands up and yelling, clambers over a desk to get to Ina in the row in front.*

V:  I'm going to make you pay for that, you cow.

T:  Vicky, go back to your desk right now.

V:  Miss, Ina called me ******** and I am going to get her.

T:  No you are not; get back to your desk right now. This is the second time this week I have had to speak to you.

V:  But Miss…

*The teacher moves towards Vicky, shouting and pointing her index finger 6 inches away from her nose…*

T:  But nothing. Sit down now and get back to work.

V:  I don't have to listen to you.

*Vicky storms out of the classroom and sneers at Ina as she leaves…*

V:  I'll get you at break.

# Mood management – situation 2

*The Teacher scans the classroom and sees Ina turning around and saying something to Vicky two rows behind.*

T:   Vicky, have you finished the assignment?

*Vicky stands up and yelling, clambers over a desk to get to Ina in the row in front.*

V    I'm going to make you pay for that, you cow.

T:   Vicky, you need to go back to your desk and complete your assignment.

V:   Miss, Ina called me ******** and I am going to get her.

T:   Vicky, I need you to sit down at your desk and get on with your assignment.

V:   But Miss…

*The teacher moves into the area between Ina and Vicky…*

T:   Vicky, I need you to sit down at your desk and get on with your assignment.

*Vicky reluctantly sits down in a huff.*

T:   Ina, a minute of your time. Can you come and talk to me at my desk? Vicky, you and I will catch up later.

# Situation 1 – analysis

The problem is not resolved in situation 1 for a number of reasons.

By saying *'Turn around now'* the teacher deals with Ina's actions and not with the main purpose of being in the classroom, which is to remind her of her work.

From here on, confrontation is enhanced by the tone of the teacher and by her bringing up another incident involving Vicky earlier in the week, which inflames the situation.

Pointing her finger in Vicky's face threatens her publicly and leads to a predictable conclusion.

Vicky at this point has lost control and the teacher, by now gambling on her authority, makes a final comment which simply fans the flames even more and leads to Vicky storming out of the room.

# Situation 2 – analysis

In situation 2 we have a different approach. It works better for the following reasons:

Initially, the impression is that the teacher is ignoring what's happening but in fact she is focusing instead on the main reason for being in the classroom, ie to do the work set.

When this does not work, the teacher shifts gear. She uses effective and non-confrontational body language by moving into the area and so defuses the incident quickly and successfully.

Finally, the teacher lets everybody know that the incident has not been ignored but that the focus at this time is on the work. By speaking to Ina first she allows Vicky some cooling off time, while showing her she realises that Ina has played a major role in the incident.

# Do's and don't's

So much of management of ODD children is about giving them 'respect' in front of their 'mates'. As a result, conversations to reinforce the correct ways of dealing with their frustrations are best done 1:1 away from the prying eyes of the rest of the group. In situations when you have to reinforce issues publicly, be aware of your body language – avoid aggressive gestures.

**Don't:**
* Shout
* Stand toe-to-toe/face-to-face
* Raise your voice in response to theirs
* Allow conflict in a public forum
* Use aggressive non-verbal communication, eg flailing arms, aggressive facial expressions
* Bring up previous incidents, eg if you are dealing with Chardonnay swearing at Chloe, stick to the issue; don't become frustrated and say, *'And another thing, you never bring in your homework'*.

# Do's and don't's

Do:

- Give ODD students the opportunity to have their say. They want to be heard and need to get the issues they feel are important **to them** off their chest
- Offer a choice of outcome and a choice of routes, either of which are OK with you, so it seems *they* have the power to make the decision and to SAVE FACE in public
- Attempt to divert their attention using distracting techniques
- Focus on the incident, not the student. Don't personalise
- Stay on the issue and don't be diverted from your objective. (See next page)

To be successful in managing students with ODD it's important not to get sidetracked by secondary behaviour issues and not to be drawn into the smokescreen – these students will try to take you there!

# How to keep on track

Use the broken record technique to keep focused on the key issue:

*'Farouk I want you to move to this seat.'*

*'But Miss, Daniel is spitting.'*

*'Farouk, I want you to move to this seat.'*

*'I can't, my stuff is not there.'*

*'Farouk, I want you to move to this seat.'*

Call it nagging, call it anything you want…it works.

# Other tips for managing ODD

There are three other useful techniques for managing students with ODD.

1.  Refer to **rights and responsibilities** and regret the sanction if faced with non-compliance. In some cases, the student with ODD will have to 'own the impact of inappropriate behaviour'. Sanctions may have to be issued in line with the rights and responsibilities section of the school's behaviour policy. Never gloat when applying a sanction; appear to issue it with a heavy sigh, eg *'It has come to this; you leave me no choice'*.
2.  Use behaviour **contracts** and **other professionals** if defiance, anger and frustration occur. Sometimes students need a more structured tool to help them measure their behaviour on a regular basis.
3.  Finally, and perhaps most important, often the best way of dealing with an angry and seemingly impossible ODD child is to **use humour**. Be careful, timing is crucial, but even in the most trying circumstances it can be the most effective strategy of all.

# Don't Care:
# CD

# Conduct Disorder

There are several key characteristics of Conduct Disorder (see Appendix 3).

Children with CD often present us with very dangerous and highly challenging behaviours. The four key areas of concern are as follows:

- Aggression to people/animals
- Destruction of property
- Deceitfulness or theft
- Serious violation of rules

According to the literature and research available, reasons for Conduct Disorder differ widely and can be attributed to both nature and nurture. One thing is certain, however: children with this condition display a range of anti-social behaviour and they are calculating in their actions.

# Conduct Disorder

Students with Conduct Disorder can be quite controlled compared with ADHD and ODD students, but, in my opinion, they're the most difficult of all to work with.

Children with Conduct Disorder are like icebergs, not because they are cold and potentially dangerous – though many of them are – but because they allow only a brief glimpse of themselves:

'It is difficult to know what Samuel knows because he won't do the work he is given, even though I feel he is capable of it. He really appears to work against some of his teachers and chooses to disrupt classes he does not enjoy. His attitude is puzzling because we feel he will not let us help him and he seems on occasion to have a different agenda.'

Head of Year 8's comment on report.

# The 3 Rs

Of the challenging behaviours children present us with, it is CD that most responds to the 3 Rs:

- **R**espect
- **R**elationships
- **R**ole models

While it is difficult to determine with certainty the reasons behind Conduct Disorder, it is clear that students who exhibit it work most effectively with people whom they believe respect them, for whatever reason.

But respect can be gained through negative as well as positive actions. We can all think of students who have the 'respect' of their peers because of their challenging behaviour. Teachers can demonstrate how CD students can earn respect for good behaviour.

# Managing CD

Children with CD are often described as anti-social because they:

*   Can be overtly and covertly aggressive
*   Consistently break rules
*   Are good at covering up

The truth is that nobody sets out to be truly anti-social; these children really need our help to work through and model good behaviour examples. It helps to remember:

*   You cannot *control* anybody's behaviour other than your own. (Children with CD are into control and so some form of compromise will be needed)
*   The way teachers behave towards any child can influence how other children relate to that individual

No half-hearted measures exist when working with these children. You have to be committed. To use a rugby analogy: players soon find out the best way to avoid injury is to tackle properly by being brave and fully committed. Anything less is potentially injurious.

# Allow them to save face

Students with CD tend to be leaders not followers, so for the 3Rs to operate in practice it is often better, even after an incident, to show some degree of restraint and positive response to a specific situation.

The language you use and how you use it is all important, as in the following examples:

- *'Even though I know you have a strong opinion regarding this issue, thank you for letting Matthew speak'*
- *'I know you think it is unfair, but thanks for letting Ruth go first'*
- *'You took notice of the idea/situation/instruction even though I can see you don't agree'*

**'It ain't what you do it's the way that you do it...**(repeat twice)
**...That's what gets results'**

# Respect

Because they like to be in charge, children with CD will try to dominate teachers and the teachers' territory. When frustrated, they may resort to a number of measures to intimidate and disrupt the teacher and to dominate the pack of other students. As a result they can appear to threaten your management of the rest of the group and – let's be honest – this means it can be difficult to actually like them.

Though it would be preferable to like all the children you work with, the truth is that it's not possible. Some students are quite difficult to like. The key is that there should be mutual respect.

# Impending conflict: signs and signals

As with ADHD and ODD, so much of CD management is reading the mood of the student and acting accordingly. Some signs to look out for:

- Unwillingness to communicate
- Looking away when you speak
- Pacing around, unwilling to remain in seat
- Outbursts of temper
- Frequent repetition of certain phrases
- Rapid speech
- False, sarcastic laughter
- Sweating, shortness of breath or rapid breathing
- Inability to settle to work
- Appearing agitated

Some students become visibly flushed or their necks redden prior to an outburst. **As usual, RED means DANGER.**

# Dealing with confrontations

When dealing with confrontations, remember the tackle theory. Successful tackling (or dealing with students' behaviour issues) is not just about WHAT you do, it's also about WHEN you do it. It's about your timing of the intervention.

> 'It is not the severity, it is the certainty.'
> **(Bill Rogers, 1996.)**

Two types of confrontation occur in classrooms – covert and overt:

| | |
|---|---|
| **1. Covert confrontation**: | student responds to you inappropriately, but others may be unaware of it. |
| **2. Overt confrontation**: | student responds to you publicly and challenges you in front of the whole group. |

Both need to be dealt with but each needs to be handled differently, especially remembering that the child with CD is trying, on most occasions, to impress his or her peers.

# Dealing with confrontations

When dealing with **covert confrontations**:

- Stay calm and in control
- Let them know you've noticed the incident but, usually, catch up with them later

When dealing with **overt confrontations**:

- Stay calm and in control
- Follow up immediately
- Use either a direct or quirky approach
- If necessary move the student away from the group

Remember never to personalise. It is the *behaviour* you don't accept *not the person*, and it's the certainty that a follow-up *will* occur that is most important, not its severity.

# Dealing with confrontations – situation 1

The Year 7 teacher hands out an assignment to each member of the class but notices that Jamie in the second row has screwed up the worksheet and is rolling it up and down the table.

T: Jamie, what do you think you are doing?

J: Having a ball what does it look like? *(Two other pupils nearby laugh)*

T: Unfold that now and get on with your work. I'm not giving you another one.

J: *(Mimics teacher quietly)* I'm not giving you another one. *(Pupils laugh again)*

T: Jamie, what did you say?  I'm warning you...

J: Warning me for what? Saying you're an idiot? You are anyway.

T: I won't be spoken to like that. Leave this class right now.

J: *(Already on his feet)* I'm already gone...*(Thinks to himself: that teacher is too easy for words)*

# Dealing with confrontations – situation 2

The Year 7 teacher hands out an assignment to each member of the class but notices that Jamie in the second row has screwed up the worksheet and is rolling it up and down the table.

T: Jamie, you can't play basketball in this class, there is no net on the wall.
*(Two other pupils laugh)*

J: *(Growling)* Get off my back and leave me alone. I'm not doing this stupid work. Not now, not ever.

T: *(Picking up the assignment in the shape of ball and aiming to shoot into the lampshade)* This is a pretty good ball but it's not heavy enough to pitch through a hoop and I should know as I'm a pretty good player – as you all know.

J: You're not that good. I'm better than you.

T: Wanna prove it? If you do this assignment, I'll play you at break. Five shots each.

J: *(Unscrewing the paper and flattening it out)* You ain't got a chance mate.
*(Thinks to himself: for a teacher he's alright I suppose)*

# Situation 1 – analysis

In this example the teacher makes a couple of critical mistakes. First, he should not have asked Jamie what he was doing. Rather, he should have found a way of directing him back to task or leading him through the motions of getting there without allowing him to lose face in front of his peers.

Instead, the initiative has been handed to Jamie who is now playing to the group. The teacher is on the back foot and compounds the error by thinking that Jamie might actually care about doing this assignment, which he clearly does not.

Jamie feels the teacher's threats are worthless and has probably already decided he wants out of the class. The teacher provides him with a route.

As with many CD students, Jamie works to his own agenda.

# Situation 2 – analysis

Here, by contrast, the teacher takes the initiative early and, though this can be risky, plays to the crowd himself by making a joke about Jamie's actions.

Jamie is now more isolated from the group and somewhat cornered. This could lead to an explosive reaction with students with ODD, but the more controlled CD child will allow the teacher to play the next move.

The teacher, either by instinct or anticipation, maintains his initial strategy but then, by slightly mocking himself, throws down another challenge to Jamie in front of the class.

Jamie is tempted by the challenge and can't resist replying.

It is then the teacher gambles on his reputation as a bit of a sportsman, something that he and Jamie have talked about in the past as a shared interest.

Jamie takes the bait for two possible reasons: either he likes the idea itself or he likes the way the teacher presented it.

# Dealing with verbal and physical abuse

It is always a good idea to have a planned response to potential flashpoint situations.

When children swear at you or use aggressive language it is tempting to become angry or upset. Though we are all human, the trick is to look behind the behaviour and remember that even though a student might be making it personal you aren't going to allow them to intimidate you and you *won't* take it personally.

In reality, while the verbal attack is aimed at you, what lies behind it is usually frustration regarding other issues. So:

* Remain calm, stop and think
* Intervene at an appropriate level
* Seek an apology
* Apply further consequences
* Reflect on the issue after the event with them and/or colleagues

The key is not to over-react. Over-reacting will inflame rather than defuse the situation.

# Dealing with verbal abuse

When incidents flare up between the CD student and other students they are usually the result of the build-up of previous issues, especially where both parties are female.

What to do:

- Interrupt and separate the children involved
- Investigate the origin of the disagreement with the pupils involved
- Investigate the incident by talking to pupils who were nearby (won't always work)
- Seek a resolution between the students involved

When both parties are male, verbal abuse is usually used as a way of mocking and of asserting position in the pack.

# Dealing with physical abuse

Fights between children actually occur fairly rarely but when they do they are usually in public and they will cause a great deal of excitement amongst the other pupils. You will be dealing with a crowd as well as the perpetrators.

- Send for help by using a student in the crowd to get another adult
- Remove the audience
- Separate the individuals as best you can
- Calm the atmosphere between the children fighting
- Follow-up what led to the incident and investigate all parties involved

This is not a sequential list, as supervisors involved will act as they see fit. Some people would want to separate the individuals first. You will need to act and react according to the specific situation.

# Managing challenging behaviours

As we have seen, dealing with individual children with challenging behaviour is most successful when you can look at the message behind the behaviour and understand the social or neurological causes.

The next chapter looks at a more general whole-school approach to dealing with a wider range of children who may not have a specific label or who occupy many areas on the behaviour spectrum.

Introduction

 The Risk Factors

 Can't Learn: ADHD

 Won't Learn: ODD

 Don't Care: CD

 The 5Ps:
Marketing
Good Behaviour ◀

 Further
Information

# The 5Ps:
# Marketing
# Good Behaviour

# The marketing model

In business the term 'marketing' is said to comprise the 5Ps:

**P**ROMOTION

**P**LACE

**P**RODUCT

**P**RICE

**P**EOPLE

Marketing, in essence, is the science or process of selling to customers.

In education we are also in the business of selling, to sometimes reluctant and unwilling children. So, can the business model be applied to teaching and managing challenging children?

What would be the ingredients of a 'marketing good behaviour' campaign?

# Promotion: rules

A key factor in promoting good behaviour is accepting responsibility. Whose responsibility is it? The answer is everybody's – teachers', students', parents'. To establish positive behaviour patterns in the large community that comprises a school, specific frameworks and systems need to be set up and promoted successfully so that *everyone* involved is clear about expectations.

The first step in the process of promoting positive behaviour is to **establish the rules** within the community. This need not be complicated. There are three crucial principles to which all stakeholders in the school (ie staff, students and parents) need to commit:

1. Consistent application of agreed behaviour rules and expectations.
2. Use of effective rewards and sanctions to support agreed rules and expectations.
3. A continuing process of developing the key behaviour rules and expectations.

# Promotion: rules

Schools will differ in how rules are produced and marketed but it is essential that they are reviewed and revised from time to time – as with any successful marketing strategy – to keep pace with changes in the community.  Ask yourself:

- Are they fresh?
- Do I have fewer than eight of them?
- Are they positively phrased?
- Are they fit for the purpose?
- Have they been agreed by *all* stakeholders?

Once the rules are agreed, a contract between all three parties should be signed and countersigned to establish the commitment towards positive behaviour.

# Promotion: rules

But it's keeping the rules that poses a major problem for children with challenging behaviour. It may be worth trying to band issues, separating those over which little or no compromise may exist from others which, though annoying and irritating, are less serious.  For example:

**Band 1**
Physical/verbal abuse
Theft
Substance abuse
Attendance/timekeeping
Dress code/phone use

**Band 2**
Disorganisation
Calling out without asking permission
Fidgeting
'Distractibility'

Any such banding needs to take into account the individual teacher, the specific child and the culture of the school. The key is that children, especially those with ADHD, ODD, CD etc, will need us to cut them some slack, possibly in Band 2. Issues in Band 1 are non-negotiable whatever the diagnostic label – yes, even if it is Pink Pyjama Syndrome.

# Place: the classroom

Playgrounds, corridors and toilets are three potential areas for incident and should have specific management and supervision policies, but most of the time children spend in school is in the classroom.

The classroom, though occupied by many, is the teacher's office and, as a result, it's for the teacher to decide what and how things run within it.

Over 20 years ago, when I was a probationary teacher, an experienced head of department gave me this advice regarding classroom management:

- Get 'em in
- Get on with it
- Get on with 'em
- Get 'em out

Simple, but valuable.

# Place: the classroom

**5Ps**

Classroom management comprises a number of principles:

- Control of students entering and leaving the room
- Good organisation of room in terms of seating, lighting, acoustics and temperature
- Clear lesson aims and objectives
- Clear communication and delivery of the lesson
- Effective time management
- Skilful management of resources
- Firmness, fairness and flexibility

# Place: the classroom

In terms of how to *'get 'em in and get 'em out'* there are various methods that work, but meeting your class at the door, starting the lesson in silence, having a seating plan, telling them how they will be expected to move about the room during this lesson and dismissing them one by one, or by tables or rows – but always on YOUR terms – is good practice.

Other things to remember:

- Have you minimised external distractions and are you aware of the danger spots?
- Can you arrange the furniture/seating plan to reduce potential trouble spots?
- Can you see them at all times and do you move around the room as opposed to sitting at your desk at the front of the class?
- Does your equipment work and do you have your materials in advance?

# Product: good behaviour

Why do some classes with challenging children run smoothly despite the number of potentially disruptive individuals?

One popular myth is that children with ADHD can't sit still in more academic classes and can only concentrate in subjects like IT and Art. In my role as a behavioural advisor I visit schools often and can say, hand on heart, I have seen ADHD children behave perfectly well in some traditionally academic classes yet be extremely disruptive in Art.

It's not the subject that makes the difference... it's the teacher.

# Product: good behaviour

What's the trick? What's the formula?
It's a combination of consistently applying common sense and the following:

- Being generally aware of challenging students and their specific needs
- Looking for patterns if and when issues occur
- Asserting the boundaries within the class
- Using the language of choice when incidents occur, eg *'Yasmin, you need to sit down, either beside Shelley or sit down at this desk beside Carlos'*
- Lesson differentiation for students who have learning issues
- Having contingency plans to remove the problem/student if necessary
- Anticipating difficulties
- Agreeing the role of the LSA – who will usually have good insight into specific students

# Product: good behaviour

* Making the class a team by getting them
  - to take pride in their environment
  - to feel safe, secure and happy
  - to assist certain students to help themselves behave positively

And remember the 3Fs: be **Firm, Fair** and **Flexible**.

FIRMNESS  FAIRNESS  FLEXIBILITY

# Product: good behaviour

When looking for patterns, consider:

1. When do the problems occur (after break, start/end of lesson, quiet time)?
2. What are the triggers (interaction with other students, boredom, particular tasks)?
3. In confrontation, how does he/she react?
4. How does your response to the student affect the outcome?
5. What seems to have a positive effect (your approach, humour, peer pressure, change of task)?

Once you establish the triggers you will be better placed to prevent them from recurring.

(An excellent resource for learning how to achieve good behaviour in lessons is the *Behaviour Management Pocketbook* by Peter Hook and Andy Vass (see page 126).)

# Price: selling good behaviour

Marketers know that, despite all their promotion and regardless of how wonderful the product is, crucial to the sale is setting an attractive price or, looking at it another way, providing incentives for the sale.

Any estate agent will tell you: *Every house has its price, and that price is what someone is willing to pay for it.*

For most traditional learners the incentive is achieving good grades, earning teacher praise and the possibility of planning for future career options. This is their motivation for buying into the idea of compliance, both in doing the work and following the rules for up to 7 hours a day, 5 days a week, 200 days a year.

For children who can't, won't or don't care, the motivation is different and so the incentives will need to be different. For that reason, looking at different options for encouraging positive performance and discouraging negative outcomes should be part of your marketing good behaviour campaign.

*Every student has their price; the skill is finding out what it is.*

# Price: selling good behaviour

So what might work as incentives?

- Positive comments
- Commendations: merits, certificates, tokens, school trips
- Contact with home
- Freedom of movement
- Video/computer options
- Choice of lessons
- Earning other responsibilities
- Specific contracted systems, eg contracts to earn phone credits, food/money, etc

As a guideline, incentives need to be achievable for all children but not so easy to earn that the currency is devalued.

# Price: selling good behaviour

A famous football manager, respected throughout the game and by his players, used to reward the best player at the end of training sessions by slipping a polo mint into their bags.

Can you imagine all those millionaires in the car park, checking their bags and being competitive about 'who got the mint today?'

*It's not what you give; it's how much you make them want it.*

# Price: selling good behaviour

Though it is true that rewards change behaviour whereas sanctions/disincentives do not usually change behaviour by themselves, they *can* buy you time to teach appropriate behaviour. Sanctions might include:

- Disappointment/displeasure of supervisor
- Loss of merits/privileges
- Removal from a specific place/class to another area
- Whole-class sanctions
- Detentions/loss of freedom of movement
- Contact with home and/or multi-agency contact

Whether it's incurring the displeasure of a respected supervisor, the loss of free time, or the awarding of special privileges, students need to feel that there are consequences – both negative and positive – for their behaviour.

This is something they understand and, ultimately, when the principle is enforced consistently it makes them feel safe and secure.

# People: parents and carers

Vital to the success of any campaign for marketing good behaviour are the parents or carers, the people who remain the greatest influence in the lives of their children. Establishing a positive relationship with them is crucial.

Yet things can break down with parents who become angry or frustrated with the school and/or individual teachers whom they perceive as picking on their child. At the heart of this is usually poor communication between school and home. To establish productive relationships you need to make frequent use of:

* Contact by telephone/text/e-mail/letter
* Parent teacher conferences
* Report cards

Remember, children with ADHD, ODD and CD can place a great deal of pressure on family relationships. Parents may require help with parenting skills and assistance to look after themselves and their children. In these cases teachers may want to refer parents to support groups such as ADDISS (**www.addiss.co.uk**), the national advocacy group for children with ADHD and related conditions.

# People: parents and carers

During meetings and/or phone conferences with parents/carers:

- Listen and acknowledge – allow them to express themselves uninterrupted
- Ask them what they think they need in order to resolve the issue
- Agree to reasonable requests. Consider who will action them and when
- Add any further elements to the solution which you feel are necessary
- Give them a clear, realistic date when you will contact them with a progress report
- Thank them and remind them that you have their child's best interest at heart

It's a good idea at the start of the meeting to set a time limit and stick to it. You can always arrange a follow-up meeting if necessary.

# People: students and teachers

The people at the heart of this campaign are the students and their teachers.
In a survey at one school, students were asked for their views on what characterised effective and ineffective teachers. Below is a summary of what they thought.

Ineffective teachers:

* Appear confused and seem uncertain about what to do when faced with bad behaviour
* Threaten and don't take action

Effective teachers:

* Won't be messed around…
* Sort out those misbehaving
* Are hard but fair with discipline
* Have clearly defined boundaries and guidelines for behaviour
* Respond in a confident manner

# People: teachers

Anger and frustration are natural responses when working with challenging children and you will feel these emotions often, both as a result of specific incidents and, perhaps, the daily grind. You will not win every battle and you will not save every child (nor should you expect to).

Never forget, however, that even if it does not always appear obvious, you **are** making a difference and that children who found the school experience difficult but who came through will usually say the reason they did so was that:

*'Someone believed in me.'*

It is not easy but neither is it impossible to help children who are unwilling, unable and quite often unhappy to become able, willing and happy.

# Further
# Information

# Appendix 1

## Attention Deficit Hyperactivity Disorder

### ADHD: Predominately Inattentive Type (A)

Six or more of the symptoms below will have persisted for at least six months in two or more environments, eg school and home, and will be inconsistent with peer behaviour.

### Inattention

- Does not appear to listen when directly addressed
- Has difficulty organising tasks and activities
- Fails to give close attention to details or makes careless errors in written work or other activities
- Struggles to sustain attention to work or play

- Does not follow through on instructions and fails to finish schoolwork or chores
- Loses necessary equipment for tasks and activities, eg books, pens, etc
- Avoids, dislikes or resists tasks that require sustained mental effort
- Forgetful
- Easily distracted

Adapted from the American Psychiatric Association's *Diagnostic and Statistical Manual of Mental Disorders IV (1994)* Pub. American Psychiatric Inc.

# Appendix 1

## Attention Deficit Hyperactivity Disorder

### ADHD: Hyperactive Impulsive Type (B)

Six or more of the symptoms below will have occurred for at least six months in two or more environments, eg school and home, and will be inconsistent with peer behaviour.

### Hyperactivity

- Often gets out of seat at inappropriate times
- Often runs about or climbs excessively at inappropriate times
- Fidgets and wriggles or squirms in seat
- Is often 'on the go' and can seem turbo-charged
- Talks excessively
- Has difficulty in playing quietly

### Impulsivity

- Has difficulty waiting his/her turn
- Prematurely blurts out answers to questions
- Regularly butts in or intrudes on others

*Adapted from the DSM IV (1994) – see foot of page 120*

# Appendix 1

## Attention Deficit Hyperactivity Disorder

### ADHD: Combined Type

Six or more symptoms are displayed in both **(A)** and **(B)**

In all cases the symptoms will have started before the child reached seven and cannot be attributable to a psychotic disorder or other mental disorder

*Adapted from the DSM IV (1994) – see foot of page 120*

# Appendix 2

## Oppositional Defiant Disorder

Negative, hostile and defiant behaviour lasting at least six months and displayed in two or more environments, eg school and home. Four or more of the following behaviours will be displayed more often than is typical for the age group.

- Deliberately defiant/refuses to comply with adults' requests or rules
- Deliberately annoys people
- Angry or resentful
- Loses temper
- Argues with adults
- Blames others for his or her mistakes or behaviour
- Touchy or easily annoyed by others
- Spiteful and vindictive

*Adapted from the DSM IV (1994) – see foot of page 120*

# Appendix 3

## Conduct Disorder

Persistent and recurring behaviour pattern which breaks rules, violates social norms, disregards the rights of others and is indicated by three or more of the criteria listed here and on page 125, displayed in the past six months.

### Aggression to people and animals

- Often bullies, threatens or intimidates others
- Often initiates physical fights
- Has used a weapon with potential to cause serious physical harm to others
- Has been physically cruel to people
- Has been physically cruel to animals
- Has stolen while confronting a victim
- Has forced someone into sexual activity

*Adapted from the DSM IV (1994) – see foot of page 120*

# Appendix 3

## Conduct Disorder

### Destruction of property
- Has deliberately destroyed other people's property
- Has deliberately started fires

### Deceitfulness or theft
- Has broken into someone else's house, building or car
- Has stolen items
- Cons others into giving goods or favours

### Serious violations of rules
- Often truants from school, beginning before age 13
- Often stays out at night in defiance of parents, beginning before age 13
- Has run away from home overnight at least twice

*Adapted from the DSM IV (1994) – see foot of page 120*

# Further Reading

**ADHD**
by F. O'Regan
Published by Continuum International, 2005

**Behaviour Management Pocketbook**
by P. Hook and A. Vass
Published by Teachers' Pocketbooks, 2004

**The Bullying Problem**
by A. Train
Published by London Souvenir Press, 1995

**Cracking the Hard Class**
by B. Rogers
Published by Paul Chapman Publishing, 1997

**Dealing with Disruptive Students**
by J. Olsen and P. Cooper
Published by Kogan Page, 2001

**Dyslexia Pocketbook**
by J. Bennett
Published by Teachers' Pocketbooks, 2006

**Educating Children with ADHD**
by P. Cooper and F. O'Regan
Published by Routledge Falmer Press, 2001

**The Explosive Child**
by R. Greene
Published by Harper Collins, 1998

**How to Teach and Manage Children with ADHD**
by F. O'Regan
Published by McGraw-Hill, 2002

**Making Sense of Behaviour**
by R. Long
Published by NASEN, 2002

# About the author

**Fin O'Regan MA, PGCE BSc**

Fin O'Regan is a former science teacher and has taught in the UK and the USA in both mainstream and specialist schools. He was headteacher of the Centre Academy – the London branch of a number of specialist schools for children with ADHD and co-morbidities based in Florida, USA – from 1996-2002. He is currently a SEN and Behaviour Consultant for the SSAT and an associate lecturer for Leicester University, the National Association for Special Needs and the Institute of Education. He is also Chairperson of the European ADHD Awareness Taskforce.

Publications include *Educating Children with ADHD* (2000); *How to Teach and Manage Children with ADHD* (2001); *Surviving and Succeeding in SEN* and *ADHD: Impact and Intervention* (both 2005); *Troubleshooting Challenging Behaviour* and *Challenging Behaviours Pocketbook* (both 2006); *Inattention, Hyperactive and Disorganised* (2008) and *Successfully Managing ADHD* (2014).

Fin can be contacted at:
www.fintanoregan.com
fjmoregan@aol.com
07734 715 378

# Order form

### *Your details*

Name _____

Position _____

School _____

Address _____

_____

_____

Telephone _____

Fax _____

E-mail _____

VAT No. (EC only) _____

Your Order Ref _____

### *Please send me:*

No. copies

Challenging Behaviours _____ Pocketbook ☐

_____ Pocketbook ☐

_____ Pocketbook ☐

_____ Pocketbook ☐

### *Order by Post*

## Teachers' Pocketbooks

Laurel House, Station Approach
Alresford, Hants. SO24 9JH  UK

### *Order by Phone, Fax or Internet*

Telephone:  +44 (0)1962 735573
Facsimile:   +44 (0)1962 733637
E-mail: sales@teacherspocketbooks.co.uk
Web: www.teacherspocketbooks.co.uk

### *Customers in USA should contact:*

2427 Bond Street, University Park, IL 60466
Tel: 866 620 6944   Facsimile: 708 534 7803
E-mail: mp.orders@ware-pak.com
Web: www.managementpocketbooks.com